THE HEART ALL LEADERS MUST DEVELOP

Cultivating the Nature of Christ

LIFE IMPACT SERIES

FRANK DAMAZIO

CityChristianPublishing

www.CityChristianPublishing.com

PUBLISHED BY CITY CHRISTIAN PUBLISHING
9200 NE Fremont, Portland, Oregon 97220

City Christian Publishing is a ministry of City Bible Church and is dedicated to serving
the local church and its leaders through the production and distribution of quality
equipping resources. It is our prayer that these materials, proven in the context of the
local church, will equip leaders in exalting the Lord and extending His kingdom.

For a free catalog of additional resources from City Christian Publishing, please call
1-800-777-6057 or visit our web site at www.citychristianpublishing.com.

The Heart All Leaders Must Develop

ISBN 13: 978-1-59383-045-8
ISBN 10: 1-59383-045-9

Cover design by DesignPoint, Inc.

All Scripture quotations, unless otherwise indicated,
are taken from The King James Version of the Bible.
In some Scripture references, italics have added by the author for emphasis.

First Edition, January 2006

Printed in the United States of America

Contents

Part 1: The Heart of a Leader..................................... 7
The term heart *has historically referred to both the physical and spiritual, the soul and mind of man—the source of human thoughts, passions, appetites, affections, and endeavors. When God asks leaders to give Him their hearts, He is requesting the core of their being, their entire lives.*

Part 2: The Heart of a Father..................................... 29
A leader with the heart of a father will strive to balance reprimand with gentleness, instruction with patience, authority with love, warning with praise, and truth with mercy.

Part 3: The Heart of a Servant 57
Jesus is the supreme example of leadership with a servant's heart. "I came to serve, not to be served," He said. Jesus similarly advised his reward-seeking apostles: "He who would be greatest among you, let him be your servant."

Part 4: The Heart of a Shepherd 81
Spiritual shepherds serve as protectors and watchmen over the flocks of God. Leaders must have the heart of a shepherd as they guide, comfort, feed, and heal the believers in their care. Again, the ultimate role model is Jesus Christ: "The Lord is my Shepherd; I shall not want."

Part 1

THE HEART OF A LEADER

At some point in your service to the Church, whatever the nature of your own ministry calling, you will probably be called to act in a leadership role. Will you qualify? Will you be ready for one of the greatest adventures of a lifetime?

While God is committed to helping you grow in faith, your level of cooperation is the releasing factor that leads to a qualified heart. He is looking for people He can trust, people who share His own heart's love and concern for the Church.

This book deals with the heart qualifications of leadership that all Christians must have: the heart of a father, the heart of a servant, and the heart of a shepherd. If you are called to a governing and equipping ministry, these are your prerequisites and the foundation of your ministry. In a congregational ministry, they are the modus operandi, the very soul of your service. They are qualities of the heart that we all rely upon to achieve our full stature as Christians.

Definition of *Heart*

What does God mean when He asks His ministers to give Him their hearts? To the Western mind, the word *heart* may generally mean (beyond the vital physical organ) the emotional feelings of a person. For example, when we in the western hemisphere say that a man loves a woman "with all of his heart," we generally mean with intense feelings.

Hebrew Meanings. To the ancient Hebrew mind, however, the meaning of *heart* encompassed not only a person's emotions, but also his spiritual, mental, and physical life. The Hebrews viewed man as a total unit, and the word *heart* was understood in that context. The Hebrew word for heart is *labab*, which in a general sense means the midst, the innermost, or the hidden parts of anything. The Bible uses such phrases as "the heart of the sea" (Exod. 15:8), "the heart of heaven" (Deut. 4:11), "the heart of a tree" (2 Sam. 18:14), and "the heart of the earth" (Matt. 12:40).

In the Hebrew, therefore, the word *heart* comes to mean, by extension, the seat of man's collective energies and the focus of his personal life. The heart would be the very throne upon which life itself sits. In relating this to the ministry, when the Lord asks a man for his heart, he wants that person to be involved in the Lord's work from the very core of his being.

Greek Meanings. In the English Bible, one of the most common Greek words that is translated as *heart* is the word *kardia*. In general meaning, *kardia* refers to the center and seat of both spiritual and physical life. It carries the connotation of both soul and mind. *Kardia* was often used to refer to the mind as the fountain and seat of human thoughts, passions, desires, appetites, affections, purposes, and endeavors. The Greek scholar H.W. Robinson believes that this Greek word (used 250 times in the New Testament) refers to the personality and the inner life and character of an individual.

From these studies, we can reach a general definition of the word *heart* as the core of a person's body, mind, emotions, personality, character, and spirit. When the Lord tells His leaders to give Him their hearts, He is asking of them their entire lives.

Importance of the Heart

Physically speaking, the heart is the most important bodily organ. Without it, the body's various organs, processes and functions would cease, and life would end. We can draw many parallels between the physical heart and the spiritual heart, showing its utmost importance in the leader's spiritual life and function:

The physical heart is located approximately in the center of a man's breast.

The spiritual heart (or the heart of the Spirit) should be located in the very center of a leader's thoughts, words, actions and ministry, motivating everything in his life.

Every physical heart is approximately the size of its owner's clenched fist.

Every leader's spiritual heart is only as big as the works of his hands show it to be.

The blood in a physical heart is composed of

different nutrients contained in the food consumed by its owner.

The life in a leader's spiritual heart is composed of what he consumes through his mind and experience. The purest life is obtained from "eating" the Word of God.

The pumping system of a physical heart is based on a reception/release method. Blood is received through one part of the heart and released through another part of the heart.

The outflowing of spiritual life from a leader is based on his own personal reception of God's love and forgiveness, and then its subsequent release to those around him.

The physical heart pumps blood from one end of the body to the other, if it is functioning properly.

The spiritual heart of a leader circulates the life of the Holy Spirit throughout the Body of Christ, if he is functioning properly.

The physical heart pumps blood throughout the body, cleansing the body from its impurities.

The spiritual heart of a leader knows and preaches the cleansing power of the blood of Jesus Christ, continually purifying the spiritual Body of Christ.

The healthy physical heart beats automatically, without the conscious effort of its owner.

The healthy spiritual heart of a leader shows the love, joy, and peace of God naturally, spontaneously, and without any conscious effort or insincere "put-on."

The physical heart is more prone to some forms of heart disease on a high-rot diet in an overweight body.

The spiritual heart of a leader is more prone to spiritual sickness as the leader takes in rich truths of the Word of God without practicing them and making them an active part of his life and the lives of others.

The physical heart is more prone to disease and attack in a body that consumes alcoholic beverages.

The spiritual heart of a leader is more prone to spiritual sickness as he dabbles with the wine of the pleasures and cares of this world.

The physical heart is more prone to disease and attack in a body that gets little exercise.

The spiritual heart of a leader is more prone to spiritual sickness the less he actually performs the will of God as expressed in God's Word.

The physical heart will be more prone to disease and attack the more tension and stress its owner experiences.

The spiritual heart of a leader is more prone to spiritual sickness as he lives a high-adrenalin, high-stress lifestyle by not entrusting all cares into the Lord's hands.

The physical heart is more prone to disease and attack the more heart defects its owner inherited from its parents at birth.

The spiritual heart of a leader is more prone to spiritual sickness the more spiritual problems he has for which he did not truly repent at the time of spiritual rebirth by the Spirit.

All of these physical parallels clearly demonstrate the importance of the spiritual heart in the life of God's leaders.

Guarding the Heart

Biblically speaking, a leader has at least three reasons to guard his heart.

The first reason is that his heart is the very source of all his attitudes and actions. We see this in the following verses:

Proverbs 4:23

"Keep thy heart with all diligence for out of it are the issues of life" (KJV).

"Keep your heart with all vigilance (and above all that you guard it) for out of it flow the springs of life" (Amplified Bible).

"Guard your heart more than any treasure, for it is the source of all life" (New English Bible).

"Above all else, guard your affections for they influence everything else in your life" (Living Bible).

Philippians 4:7

"The peace of God which passeth all under-standing shall keep your hearts and minds through Christ Jesus" (KJV).

"The peace of God which transcends all under-standing shall garrison and mount guard over your hearts and minds" (Amplified Bible).

In these passages, the leader is exhorted to guard his heart as a soldier guards the city gate. The leader must watch over his affections to prevent an invasion of foreign values. He must maintain the alertness and discipline of a sentinel who guards over a camp or castle to protect his king within.

The second reason a leader must guard his heart is because it is the source of all that he ministers or speaks. We see this in Matthew 12:34b-35.

"Out of the abundance of the heart, the mouth speaketh" (KJV).

"Out of the fullness, the overflow, the superabundance of the heart, the mouth speaketh. The good man from his inner treasure flings forth good things, and the evil man out of his inner evil storehouse flings forth evil things" (Amplified Bible).

Each leader is the guard in charge of the storehouse of his own heart, which is full of either good or bad treasures. It is out of this storehouse that the leader brings forth good or evil to the open treasure boxes of the people of the Lord. The Old Testament provides some beautiful illustrations of this. In the history of Israel, many storehouses full of grain, wine, oil, or weapons were designated for the benefit and protection of the people. Both Solomon and Hezekiah were very proud of the wealth in their storehouses (1 Kings 9:19; 2 Chron. 32:28).

In the same way, every leader must ask himself if he is proud of the contents of the storehouses of his heart. From them, he must feed and protect the people of the Lord. Solomon stored grain, wine, oil, and weapons for the defense of Israel. Today, the spiritual leader must store in his heart the Word of God, the joy of the Lord, the anointing of the Spirit, and the full armor of God (Eph. 6:13-17).

The third reason a leader must guard his heart is to prevent it from causing spiritual defilement to himself or God's people. You can see this in the words of Jesus:

And when he had called all the people unto him, he said unto them, "Hearken unto me every one of you, and understand: there is nothing from without a man, that entering into him can defile him: but the things which come out of him, those are they that defile the man. If any have ears to hear, let him hear." And when he was entered into the house from the people, his disciples asked him concerning the parable. And he said unto them, "Are ye so without understanding also? Do ye not perceive, that whatsoever thing from without entereth into the man it cannot defile him: because it entereth not into his heart, but into his belly and goeth out into the draught, purging all meats?" And He said, "That which cometh out of a man, that defileth the man. For from within, out of the heart of men, proceed evil thoughts, adulteries, fornications, murders, thefts, covetousness, wickedness, deceit, lasciviousness, an evil eye, blasphemy, pride, foolishness: all these evil things come from within, and defile the man" (Mark 7:14-23, KJV).

The Lord Jesus Christ said that the unguarded heart of a leader can become the source for a long list of terrible things: base and wicked thoughts, sexual immorality, murders, stealing, covetous desires, dangerous and destructive wickedness, unrestrained and indecent conduct, an eye that looks for evil, an abusive mouth that slanders and makes malicious misrepresentations, a heart that is uplifted in pride against God and man, and a reckless love of folly.

It is the tragedy of the Church that at some

periods in its history, this list of shame has become the agenda for some of its most influential leaders. What went wrong? Both the leaders and those who followed them left their hearts unguarded. Instead of shepherding God's flock, these leaders were foremost among those who "like sheep have wandered away." Grazing from one pleasure to another, they have lost all track of God's will for the Church.

Qualities of the Heart

Thus we see that the qualities of a leader's heart are very important to God. God is continually trying (Deut. 8:2), searching (Jer. 17:10), and pondering (Prov. 21:2) the hearts of His leaders. It is a leader's responsibility to maintain a pure heart before the Lord (Jas. 4:8).

What's the condition of your heart? In large part, that will be determined by your reaction to the Lord, to people and events around you. When you see a big need in someone's life, do you have a willing heart to help? Or do you have a hardened heart that says, "This just can't be fixed"? When the Lord confronts you with your own sin, do you have a tender heart? Or do you have a hypocritical heart that says, "Please, Lord, not now. I'm in the middle of something important. Could we just straighten it out later"? When you hear an inspiring scriptural truth in a good sermon, do you have a retaining heart that makes plans to implement the truth later in the week? Or do you have a double heart that enjoys the thrill of discovering a new idea but fails to follow through with action?

This chart of "Spiritual Heart Qualities" contains a list of heart qualities with Bible verses describing both the positive and negative sides to each quality. This is an excellent tool for evaluating the condition of your own heart. Through the Spirit and the Word, God can use it to help you pinpoint and adjust any unhealthy conditions in your spirit. If you are or desire to be a church leader, it should be part of your "spiritual curriculum." Anyone will profit by reading and praying through the list. The list of positive qualities is a distilled inspirational message from God's Word.

Spiritual Heart Qualities

Positive

Grieved Heart	Gen. 6:6
Willing Heart	Exod. 25:2
Stirred Heart	Exod. 35:21
Wise Heart	Exod. 35:35
Perfect Heart	1 Chron. 12:38
Tender Heart	2 Chron. 34:27
Sorrowful Heart	Neh. 2:2-12
Faithful Heart	Neh. 9:8

Positive

Soft Heart	Job 23:16
Upright Heart	Job 33:3
Communing Heart	Ps. 4:4
Heart of Wax	Ps. 22:14
Pure Heart	Ps. 24:4
Broken Heart	Ps. 34:18
Panting Heart	Ps. 38:10
Failing Heart	Ps. 40:12
Proclaiming Heart	Ps. 45:1
Fixed Heart	Ps. 57:7
Living Heart	Ps. 69:32
Established Heart	Ps. 112:8
Understanding Heart	Prov. 2:2
Retaining Heart	Prov. 4:4, 21
Sound Heart	Prov. 14:30
Merry Heart	Prov. 17:22
New Heart	Ezek. 18:31, 36:26
Fleshly Heart	Ezek. 11:19

Purposeful Heart	Dan. 1:8
Pondering Heart	Luke 2:19
Forgiving Heart	Matt. 18:35
Unblameable Heart	1 Thess. 3:13
Blood-sprinkled Heart	Heb. 10:22
Nourished Heart	Jas. 5:5
Sanctified Heart	1 Pet. 1:22
Assured Heart	1 John 3:19
Honest, Good Heart	Luke 8:15
Burning Heart	Luke 24.25-32
Single Heart	Acts 2:46
One Heart	Acts 4:32
Opened Heart	Acts 16:14
Obedient Heart	Rom. 6:17
Circumcised Heart	Rom. 2:29
Believing Heart	Rom. 10:9, 10
Steadfast Heart	1 Cor. 7:37
Enlarged Heart	1 Cor. 6:11
Caring Heart	1 Cor. 8:16

| Singing Heart | Eph. 5:19 |
| Established Heart | Heb. 13:9 |

Negative

Evil Heart	Gen. 6:5
Hardened Heart	Exod. 4:21
Deceived Heart	Deut. 11:16
Non-Perceiving Heart	Deut. 29:4
Presumptuous Heart	Esther 7:5
Hypocritical Heart	Job 36:13
Lifted-up Heart	Deut. 8:14
Firm, Hard Heart	Job 41:24
Iniquitous Heart	Ps. 41:6
Wicked Heart	Ps. 58:2
Erring Heart	Ps. 95:10
Proud Heart	Ps. 101:5
Fat and Greasy Heart	Ps. 119:70
Desolate Heart	Ps. 143:4
Despising Heart	Prov. 5:12

Deceitful Heart	Prov. 12:20
Bitter Heart	Prov. 14:10
Backslidden Heart	Prov. 14:14
Foolish Heart	Prov. 15:7
Human Heart	Prov. 15:11
Abominable Heart	Prov. 26:25
Double Heart	Jas. 1:8
Wounded Heart	Ps. 109:22
Evil Heart	Matt. 15:19
Rebellious Heart	Jer. 5:23
Arrogant Heart	Isa. 9:9
Deceitful Heart	Jer. 17:9
Whorish Heart	Ezek. 6:9
Stony Heart	Ezek. 11:19
Weak Heart	Ezek. 16:30
Despiteful Heart	Ezek. 25:15
Bitter Heart	Ezek. 27:31
Beastly Heart	Dan. 4:16
Divided Heart	Hos. 10:2

Negative

Hard Heart	Matt. 13:15
Heavy Heart	Prov. 31:6
Reasoning Heart	Mark 2:6-8
Envious, Striving Heart	Jas. 3:14
Lustful Heart	Ps. 81:12
Troubled Heart	John 14:1
Uncircumcised Heart	Acts 7:51
Darkened Heart	Rom. 1:21
Hard, Impenitent Heart	Rom. 2:5
Anguished Heart	1 Cor. 2:4
Blind Heart	Eph. 4:18
Unknowing Heart	Heb. 3:10
Evil Heart	Heb. 3:12
Condemning Heart	1 John 3:20
Overwhelmed Heart	Ps. 61:2
Evilly-exercised Heart	2 Pet. 2:14

Part 2

THE HEART OF A FATHER

Greek meanings. "For though ye have ten thousand instructors in Christ, yet have ye not many fathers" (1 Cor. 4:15).

In the original Greek language, the word for instructor meant "a boy leader, tutor, guide, guardian, or servant whose office it was to take the children to school." Among the Greeks and the Romans, an instructor could also be a trustworthy servant or steward who was charged with supervising the lives and morals of boys in the higher classes of society. The boys were not allowed to step out of the house without their instructor until they reached the age of manhood. The word carried with it the idea of severity; an instructor was a stern censor and enforcer of proper morals for the young men.

This Pauline verse uses the word instructor to present a strong contrast. Paul wrote to the Corinthian Christians that they had many tutors or instructors (those who freely offered them strict teaching and rigid rules) but not many fathers. The word instructor denotes a student-teacher relationship of instruction, whereas the word father denotes a father-son relationship of love. The Book of Proverbs was built on this concept of the father-son relationship. The father's wisdom, knowledge, and understanding of life is transmitted to the son in a loving father-son relationship.

Hebrew Meanings. The voice in much of Proverbs is that of the father speaking to his son. It illustrates the attitude of a father's heart:

"My son, hear the instruction of thy father" (1:8).

"My son, if sinners entice thee, consent not" (1:10).

"My son, walk not thou in the way with them" (1:15).

"My son, if thou wilt receive my words" (2:1).

"My son, forget not my law" (3:1).

"My son, despise not the chastening of the Lord" (3:11).

"My son, let them not depart from thy eyes, keep sound wisdom" (3:21).

"My son, attend to my words, incline thy ears to my sayings" (4:20).

"My son, keep thy father's commandment" (6:20).

The Church Today

As in Paul's day, so it is true in our day, that the Church has 10,000 instructors, but not nearly as many fathers. The Church has many scholars and professional ministers, but not nearly as many spiritual fathers. Many scholars and professional ministers in the Church today can deliver eloquent, impressive sermons that touch our minds and thoughts. But where are the fathers? Some religious colleges and seminaries today seem bent on mass-producing teachers. But who is attempting to produce spiritual fathers?

Will the Church allow a leadership of orators, educators, and instructors to forever rob her of the spiritual blessings which only spiritual fathers can bring her? The world has the service of thousands of erudite scholars, but the Church is still crying out for the ministry of true spiritual fathers. The Church does not need any more computer-like men with memory banks full of dry biblical information to instruct the unlearned in the ways of the Lord. She needs true spiritual fathers who can lead her in the ways of the Lord. The Church needs men who have a heart for the people of the Lord and a compassion for the needy.

A computer presents information without love, mercy, or understanding. A leader will show as much love, mercy, or understanding as a computer shows, if he does not have the heart of a father. The Church needs more than just biblical knowledge or instruction. She needs the very heart and life of her spiritual fathers to be imparted to her. The impartation of spiritual life, however, can't be taught from a college textbook in a college classroom. Spiritual life can only be learned in a close relationship with God, God's people, and the spiritual example of true fathers in the faith.

The Father's Heart of Jesus

Let's first look at the characteristics of a father's heart in the life of the ultimate example to all leaders, the Lord Jesus Christ. Jesus was the full expression of the heart of the heavenly Father on earth. His words, His ways, and His actions all manifested the heart of the Father. Accordingly, Jesus said, "I and the Father are one" (John 10:30) and "He who has seen me has seen the Father; how do you say 'Show us the father?'. . . .The Father abiding in me does His works" (John 14:9c, 10c). The list below shows some of the father's-heart attitudes of the Lord Jesus Christ, who is the role model to all of God's leaders.

Compassion. "When he saw the multitude, he was moved with compassion" (Matt. 9:35, 36).

Concern. A Pharisee asked one of Christ's disciples, "Why eatest your master with publicans and with sinners?" and Jesus replied, "They that be whole need not a physician, but they that are sick" (Matt. 9:11-13).

Willingness. "There came a leper and worshipped him, saying, 'Lord, if thou wilt, thou canst make me clean.' And Jesus put forth his hand and touched him, saying, 'I will; be thou clean' " (Matt. 8:1-3).

Humility. Jesus gave us a new definition of humility: "Except ye be converted as a little child, ye shall not enter the kingdom of heaven" (Matt. 18:3; Phil. 2:5-10).

Warmth. "Mary has chosen the better part," Jesus said to Martha, in explaining why Mary shouldn't have to leave her listeners' place at the feet of Jesus to busy herself with service (Luke 10:38-42; John 12:1-8).

Forgiveness. Jesus also gave us a new definition of forgiveness. On the cross: "Father, forgive them for they know not what they do" (Luke 23:34). In the tale of the prodigal son: "When the son was a great way off, his father saw him and had great compassion on him and ran and embraced him, and kissed him" (Luke 15:32). To a prostitute taken in sin: "Neither do I condemn you; go and sin no more" (John 8:11).

Brokenness. Jesus laid down all His heavenly authority in coming to earth, and was the model of brokenness for all leaders. "He groaned in his spirit and was troubled . . . and Jesus wept" (John 11:33-36). "O Jerusalem, Jerusalem," He lamented, "how often would I have gathered thy children together, even as a hen gathereth her chickens under her wings, and ye would not!" (Matt. 23:37).

Self-Sacrifice. Jesus showed us how to pay the ultimate price. "I lay down my life for the sheep" (John 10:15).

Service. Jesus also showed us that no service

was unimportant or without dignity. "If I then, your Lord and Master, have washed your feet, ye also ought to wash one another's feet" (John 13:14).

Fatherly Gentleness

In 1 Thessalonians 2:7, Paul states, "But we were gentle among you." In the Amplified Bible, this verse reads, "But we behaved gently when we were among you, like a devoted mother nursing and cherishing her own children."

The word *gentle* in the original Greek means to be affable, mild, or kind. Greek writers frequently used this word to characterize a nurse with crying children or a teacher with difficult pupils. This word describes a nursing mother.

Gentleness is another attitude to be found in the heart of a father. Gentleness describes the loving, fatherly touch that all children must have during their development. Without this gentleness, children will be imbalanced. The Bible requires gentleness of all those who are going to take responsibility in the house of the Lord. Without gentleness, a strong leader will injure the people of God.

This list of scriptural references on gentleness will exhort every leader to allow the Lord to develop this quality in his life.

2 Tim. 2:24: "The servant of the Lord must not strive but be gentle," Paul told his disciple Timothy.

Titus 3:2: "They are not to be brawlers, but to be gentle."

Jas. 3:17: "But the wisdom from above is first pure, peaceable, gentle."

2 Cor. 10:1: "I, Paul beseech you by the meekness and gentleness of Christ."

Gal. 5:22: "The fruit of the Spirit is . . . longsuffering, gentleness, goodness and faith."

A spiritual father in the house of the Lord must develop gentleness. This heart attitude will allow the leader to teach sensitive and difficult subjects in the Church without spiritually hurting or permanently offending the people of God. Gentleness will cause the people to listen and to respond to the more serious admonitions that a leader feels he must give.

Fatherly Nursing

1 Thessalonians 2:7 states, "but we were gentle among you, even as a nurse cherisheth her children." In the New Testament Greek, a nurse nourishes children to the point of fattening them, cherishing them with choice foods. This word denotes a mother who nurses her children before they are weaned. It describes the mother who would take the most anxious and tender care of her little ones.

In the context of this scripture, we have the

apostle Paul speaking to a church he had begotten in the gospel. In the next verse (1 Thess. 2:8), Paul described the outworking of a father's heart. He said, "So being affectionately desirous of you, we were willing to have imparted unto you, not the gospel of God only, but also our own souls, because ye were dear unto us."

The apostle Paul imparted to the Thessalonians not only the gospel, but his own life and energy as well. What Paul gave to these Christians can be seen in the feelings expressed by a mother who nurses her own child. This is the true picture of a "nursing father," in the masculine sense, as it relates not only to the apostle Paul, but also to every leader.

Acts 13:18 gives us an account of how the Lord nursed His people Israel in Old Testament times. This verse states, "God suffered their manners in the wilderness." The Septuagint translation puts it this way: "God bare, as a nursing Father, the people of Israel." Similarly, Deuteronomy 1:31 states, "In the wilderness where thou hast seen that the Lord my God bare thee as a man doth bare his son."

The Hebrew word for bare means to build up, support, foster (as a parent), to nurse, or render firm or faithful in all dealings. Numbers 11:12 speaks of Moses in this sense of the word. Moses was a nursing father to the Israelites (Isa. 40:11 and 49:23).

For all that the nation of Israel did to offend the Lord, He was still patient with them and cared for them. He was a nursing father unto the people. Moses was a nursing father to Israel also. This attribute of being like a nurse was worked into the life of Moses through all of the experiences of the people of Israel. Moses never wanted to trade Israel for a better nation, though the Lord proposed it. Moses never asked the Lord to judge them too harshly. He was a true father-nurse. May it be the same with every leader.

Fatherly Cherishing

Paul stated that he treated the Thessalonian Christians "as a nurse cherisheth her children." The Septuagint uses this word to describe a bird caring for its young by spreading its feathers over them in the nest (Deut. 22:6; Matt. 23:37).

A spiritual father in the family of God will spread his protective and loving wings over the small or weak of the flock while they are still in the nest, to protect them from the attacks of vultures. This is another expression of the father's heart in the work of leading (1 Thess. 2:8, 11; Phil. 2:22; 1 Tim. 3:1; Eph. 5:29). We think of leading as handling adults adroitly and running a "tight ship." But God thinks of leading as nursing, caring, being gentle, serving, teaching, and loving children.

The Example of Husbandry

The tender care and feeding of a young plant so

that it grows properly to a healthy maturity is another beautiful illustration of the words gentleness, nursing, and cherishing.

Plants may suffer from many different maladies during their lives. They may suffer from vegetation diseases, insect damage, environmental changes, or damage from sheer neglect. Some plants are more tender than others. Some will suffer severely by neglect, while others will appear to thrive on it. But even an old sturdy standby plant can be affected drastically by neglect or environmental change.

A plant's appearance and growth indicate the state of its health. Early stages of ailment and ill health are usually very subtle. Unless the gardener knows the plant through close relationship, he will not discern the problem until devastating symptoms occur. Stages of severe defoliation and withering are not the time for the gardener suddenly to examine the plant for causes of ill health. Unfortunately, this kind of emergency help is found too often in the vineyard of God's people!

To prevent his plants from reaching a state of emergency, the gardener must discern the need of the plant in its early stages. In doing so, the gardener will save his plant from death—and perhaps others around it. The husbandman must use preventative measures to ensure the health of his vineyard.

Applying the wrong therapy to any plant problem is very wasteful. And if the supposed remedy is too strong, the plant might not survive it. As a discerning father, the husbandman must be alert to meet the various needs of his plants. Some plants will need to be re-potted. For others, re-potting could be a sure end. Some plants need more room for their roots to reach maturity. Others need their roots trimmed and even to be put into a smaller pot. Needs vary, and rule-of-thumb gardening simply doesn't work.

Some plants may appear very beautiful on the surface, but beneath the soil have rotten and dead roots. Surprisingly enough, over-watering can cause this. A husbandman may also kill his plants by too much exposure to sunlight. Every plant needs water and sunlight in different amounts. To meet every plant's needs according to its nature and level of maturity requires a wise and experienced husbandman.

All that can be said of the natural elements of plant husbandry can also be said of leading the children of the Lord. A father-hearted Christian leader will discern and minister to the different needs and maturity levels of the people of God. This ability is the fruit of a father's gentle, cherishing, and nursing heart of love. The following chart on "Spiritual Husbandry" illustrates the parallels between husbandry and spiritual leadership.

Spiritual Husbandry Principles

The Wise and Experienced Husbandman Gives to the Plants:

Sunlight

Water

Cultivation

Pruning

Proper environment

New pot and soil

Treatment for ailments

Early detection of disease

Room for growth

Husbandry Principles

The Father-Hearted Leader Gives to the People of God:

Light of God's Word

Water of God's Spirit

Training for ministry

Fatherly discipline

Proper church atmosphere of God's presence

New lifestyle in Christ

Help and counsel for problems

Observation of any problems in their early
stages

Room to grow and exercise ministry

Spiritual Husbandry Application

A spiritual husbandman, who has a father's heart, will therefore pursue the following practices in caring for God's people:

- Provide the spiritual nourishment for balanced Christian growth
- Deal tenderly with the people of the Lord
- Discern the needs of the children of God at any stage of their development
- Be gentle and loving in relationships with

the people of the Lord

- Consistently attend to the spiritual, emotional, physical, or mental needs of the children of God

Fatherly Nurture and Admonition

Ephesians 6:4 effectively expresses the fatherly attitudes of nurture and admonition:

"Ye fathers, provoke not your children to wrath, but bring them up in the nurture and admonition of the Lord" (KJV).

The Amplified Bible translates this verse:

"Fathers, do not irritate and provoke your children to anger—do not exasperate them to resentment—but rear them (tenderly) in the training and discipline and counsel and admonition of the Lord."

In this chapter, the apostle Paul was teaching about raising a family. He was giving principles a father must follow in bringing up his children. The attitudes and principles a natural father needs to raise his natural children are those a spiritual father needs in raising his spiritual children. The house of the Lord needs these guidelines to rear its children in a balanced way. Paul used two words, *nurture* and *admonition*, to illustrate this balance.

A study of the Greek word for *nurture* brings out an entirely different meaning than we find in today's English. In the New Testament Greek, the word *nurture* meant to promote the development of a child by teaching, supporting, and encouraging him during the different stages of his growth. It meant to tutor or educate a child by training, discipline, or correction. To nurture was to chastise with the intent of molding character into the child. The word included the idea of training and educating children, of cultivating their minds and/or morals by correcting and reproving them with words and actions.

Nurture. The word *nurture* is translated several different ways in the KJV, with three primary forms being instruction, learning, and chastening (2 Tim. 3:16; 1 Tim. 1:20; 2 Tim. 2:25; Heb. 12:5; Acts 7:22; Rev. 3:19).

Jesus illustrates the heart attitude of nurturing in His teaching. The Lord Jesus was a man of true love and compassion for all people. This did not stop Him from speaking the truth in a way that sometimes offended many people. He offended not only the hypocritical religious leaders of Israel, but also His own disciples (Matt. 15:12, Mark 14:27 and John 6:60-62). In the New Testament, nurture does not mean gently nursing to maturity, but the strong teaching a child needs to mature in the Lord.

In Ephesians 6:4, Paul was not focusing on a father's love for his children, though that was not absent from the verse. Paul was focusing on the responsibility of a father to teach his children. Paul was giving an important charge to fathers: if they desire to raise their children correctly, they must have the "heart and the hand" to teach them in a very firm manner.

The ministry of a spiritual father includes strong teaching. A true spiritual father must be prepared to strongly correct his spiritual children. He must mold the character of the child through teaching that is hard and grievous for the child at times but that is still necessary. The word *nurture* that Paul used in Ephesians 6:4 was not the tender word that many people think it was. Today, the Church desperately needs spiritual fathers who have the courage to nurture her to full maturity by discipline, correction, and chastening.

Admonition. The word translated *admonition* in Ephesians 6:4 meant calling attention to something by mild rebuke, warning, and exhortation (as from the Lord). Literally, it meant putting into the mind. The word involved training by verbal encouragement, or, if necessary, verbal reproof and remonstrance. The Greek word translated as *admonition* or warning is *noutheto*. The following list of scriptures shows the different ways in which the New Testament translates this word:

Acts 20:31 – "ceased not to warn every man night and day"

Rom. 15:4 – "able to admonish one another"

1 Cor. 4:14 – "but as my beloved sons, I warn you"

Col. 3:16 – "admonishing one another in psalms and hymns"

1 Thess. 5:12 – "those that admonish you"

Admonition is a strong disciplinary word describing a very important attitude of a spiritual father. A spiritual father must put into the mind of the child the teachings that he alone knows the child needs for spiritual development and a healthy future. It takes constant exhortation and strong encouragement in righteousness to reach this goal.

All spiritual fathers in the Lord must decide to admonish. God's children need strong rebuke at times to reach maturity. Many teachers today would prefer to teach only what is pleasing and will keep people coming back. That is not always what people need. A spiritual father must discern the precise needs of God's people. Through strong exhortation and teaching, he must impart it to them.

A Balanced Father's Heart

Every leader must balance the heart attitudes of a spiritual father that have been presented in this chapter. Nurture and admonition must stay in balance with gentleness, nursing, and cherishing. Nurture and admonition are strong words which describe a leader's ministry of correction and discipline to God's people. These are needed, but are incomplete by themselves. The people of the Lord will not respond to the leader who speaks only rebuke and warning, who has hardened his heart in a one-sided pursuit of discipline. God's leaders must weep with the people. They must feel their burdens and heavy hearts in order to minister effectively. Gentleness, love, mercy, and warmth must go with discipline.

The life of the apostle Paul demonstrates all of these attitudes. His ministry, a powerful one, was not composed exclusively of rebuke, chastisement, and discipline. He also had a heart of gentleness, love, mercy, and compassion.

The following chart depicts the balance of discipline and love each leader must maintain in his ministry. If developed, both of these important sides of a leader's life will together maintain balanced growth for the Church.

Admonition	⟷	Gentleness
Instruction	⟷	Nourishment
Correction	⟷	Forgiveness
Chastisement	⟷	Patience
Authority	⟷	Love
Rebuke	⟷	Kindness
Warning	⟷	Praise
Truth	⟷	Mercy
Judgment	⟷	Justice

The heart of a spiritual father normally appears only in older people. Both years and experience are required to develop its characteristics. A younger person gains a father's heart only through early cultivation of certain attitudes and principles in his life.

In our day, many groups emphasize the academic and social preparation of a leader. The Bible, however, puts a far greater emphasis on the character and attitudinal preparation of a leader. It is possible to prepare a person's intellect for the ministry without preparing a person's heart. To successfully lead in a governmental ministry, a leader must have a prepared heart. The person who desires to help the people of God mature spiritually will seek God's help in developing the heart attitudes of a spiritual father.

Part 3

THE HEART OF A SERVANT

A leader, most people would say, is a person who directs, administrates, organizes, makes decisions, delegates responsibilities, and plans for the future. This definition lacks a very essential part of true leadership: a leader is one who serves. A leader of God's people must have the inner attitudes and motivations, and the outer service, of a servant.

Hebrew Meanings

The Old Testament translates several Hebrew words as servant. Each presents a certain portion of truth concerning the heart of a servant.

Ebed. Our first Hebrew word for servant, *ebed*, generally means a slave or a servant. It is used in several applications, all of which apply quite well to a definition of a ministry of leadership.

Ebed applies to a person who is at the complete disposal of another person (Gen. 24:1-67). A leader of God's people must be at the complete disposal of the Lord Jesus Christ and of those whom he is called to serve.

A person who works for a master is also described as *ebed* (Deut. 15:12-18). In the same way, a leader must work for his master the Lord Jesus Christ. All his work is offered as a labor to Christ, and also to those whom he is called to serve.

This word also applies to a slave who has given up all of his personal rights to serve his master (Deut. 15:12-18). A Church leader must give over all his personal rights to the Lord Jesus Christ, and to those whom he is called to served.

An *ebed* is also a slave in the service of a king (1 Kings 1:9, 47). A Christian leader must be a love-slave of the Lord Jesus Christ, who is the king above all earthly kings.

Finally, this word also applies to a person who serves in attendance to the temple sanctuary (1 Sam. 3:9). A Christian leader must tend the true temple of God, the Church, with his worship toward God and his service to God's people. (For further studies on ebed, see Gen. 26:15, 24 and 32:45; Num. 12:7; Deut. 7:8; Josh.1:1, 2, 13, 15 and 24:29; 1 Sam. 3:9, 10 and 29:3; Isa. 20:3 and 49:3; Jer. 33:22; Joel 2:29; Zech. 1:6 and 3:8.)

Abad. Another Hebrew word for servant, *abad*, generally means to work and to serve. This word also has a variety of applications which help define Church leadership.

A person who tills the ground is an *abad* (Gen. 2:5; 3:23). A leader of God's people must work at breaking up the fallow ground of their hearts so that they can receive the seed of the Word of God.

This word also applies to a person who dresses or keeps a garden (Gen. 2:15). A leader of the Church must dress and keep God's vineyard, the Church of Jesus Christ.

The name of *abad* also applies to a priest who serves the people (Num. 18:7, 23). A Christian leader must lay down his life in sacrificial service to those whom God has called him to serve.

(For further studies on *abad*, see Exod. 23:25; Deut. 4:19, 28; Josh. 22:5, 27; 1 Sam. 12:14, 20; Ps. 22:30 and 72:11; Joel 2:22, 23; Jer. 34:14; Ezek. 29:20 and 36:9; Mal. 3:18.)

Sakiyr. A third Hebrew word for servant, *sakiyr*,

generally means a person who works for wages by day or by year. This word has a variety of useful applications in defining conditions of Church leadership.

The *sakiyr*, as a hired servant, could not eat the Passover of his master's family (Exod. 12:3-45). A leader of the Church must forsake the attitude of "paid professionalism." To eat of the true Passover lamb, Jesus Christ, he must by faith enter into the relationship of love slave to the Lord, rather than paid servant.

The hired servant was not a love slave (Lev. 25:39-42). A Christian leader must come to a point in his life where he forsakes a religion of legalism that protects his rights. He must move into a personal relationship with God through faith in Jesus Christ, where his total self is given in exchange for Christ.

A *sakiyr* was not worth half of the amount that a love slave was worth (Deut. 15:18). A leader must realize that ministry and activities not motivated by the love of God are not worth half as much as those motivated out of a love relationship.

A *sakiyr* may also be a sojourner who is taken into a house as a slave (Lev. 25:6). A leader of the Church must recognize that he was once only a wandering stranger before Jesus Christ bought him with His own blood and established him in the house of God. (Other scriptures which use the word sakiyr are Exod. 22:14, 15; Lev. 19:13 and 22:10 and 25:40, 50, 53.)

Sharath. A fourth Hebrew word for servant, *sharath*, usually means a person who is a doer of menial and insignificant tasks.

A priest who ministers or serves in his priestly office is called a *sharath* (Exod. 28:35-43). A leader of the Church must perform seemingly insignificant tasks to fulfill his role as a servant-priest.

This word also applies to a priest who ministers

continually before the ark of the covenant (1 Chron. 16:37). A leader is held responsible to continually receive power for service by entering into the presence of the Lord with praise and worship.

Joshua was a *sharath* to Moses (Exod. 24:13; Num. 11:28) A leader of God's people has authority only as he is under proper authority, serving those over him with a servant's heart.

Greek Meanings

The New Testament uses a Greek word for servant, *doulos*, which gives us a very good word picture of a servant's heart. Generally, doulos signifies bondage, but most commonly applies to a servant who has willingly bonded himself to a master, by some legal obligation. Paul the apostle uses this word to describe himself in several of his epistles:

Rom. 1:1   "Paul a servant *(doulos)* of Jesus Christ."

Phil. 1:1   "Paul a servant *(doulos)* of
                   Jesus Christ."

Titus 1:1   "Paul a servant *(doulos)* of
                   God."

The Love Slave

The Old Testament provides the Hebrew background for this concept in Deuteronomy 15:1-23. When it came time for a master to release a slave after six years of service, according to the Mosaic Covenant, the slave had two options. The slave could accept his total freedom with no legal obligations to his master or he could stay in his master's house as a love slave. If he chose to stay in his master's house as a love slave, he was far more valuable to his master than the slaves who worked only to fulfill a debt or some other legal obligation. The servant who became a love slave said to his master, in essence, "Because it is well with me as your slave, and because I love you and your household, I will serve you forever on the basis of my deep love for you."

Paul was this kind of a servant of the Lord Jesus Christ. He, like any other leader of the Church, was bought with the price of the blood of Jesus Christ. He realized he could never pay back this debt by working with a "for-hire" mentality. He desired nothing less than a relationship where his work and service was motivated purely from willingness and love.

The most effective leaders in the kingdom of God are those who serve the Lord only out of a desire to love Him. Such leaders do not serve for money, reputation, position, power, or selfish advantage, even though their service means long hours of pressure and sacrifice. The leader with a servant's heart, who is secure in his personal relationship with the Lord and does not have to prove himself, is able to serve sincerely with no desire for personal profit or fame.

The New Testament Concept of Serving

Several Greek words in the New Testament present the concept of serving. From these several Greek words, the English word most commonly used is the word deacon. Today, a large portion of the Church world does not properly understand the New Testament concept of deaconship or servanthood.

Some people erroneously think deaconship is limited to a small group of worthies in the local church who take the offering or serve communion. They believe it is the mere conferral of a title for the performance of some symbolic religious functions. But the true meaning of deaconship goes far deeper. The early Church appointed men as deacons only after they already manifested the qualities of a deacon: a good reputation, being full of the spirit, and being full of wisdom (Acts 6:3). Before recognition as deacons, they had to be functioning in the requirements of the office already.

First, a Servant. Any leader, moreover, must first be a deacon (servant) in the true sense of the word. On the basis of servanthood, he is able to lead. The ministries of Jesus and His apostles were all founded on a servant's "people-conscious" heart. Jesus said that he came to serve, not to be served (Mark 10:45; Luke 22:27). He told his ambitious, position-seeking apostles that "He that would be greatest among you, let him be your servant" (Matt. 23:11). To every leader, Jesus is the supreme example of servanthood.

Today, however, some leaders would still repeat the selfish words of some of Jesus' disciples, who said, "Master, do what we desire" and "Grant that we may sit on your right and left hand in your kingdom" (Matt. 20:20-28). The selfish disciples desired a position for themselves, but there is no room for such an attitude in any of Christ's leaders.

Christ's leaders must desire to serve, not to be served, to give, and not to take. They must find true happiness in pleasing God and the Church. To put one's own happiness first would violate the heart of a servant. Selfishness is contrary to the law of the love-slave (Rom. 1:1; Deut. 15:1-23). It is contrary to the laws of promotion in God's kingdom (Matt. 23:12), love (1 Cor. 12:4-6), eternal life (Luke 10:25-27), wisdom (Prov. 22:9), the Gospel (Luke 9:24-26), and humility (Phil. 2:3-5; 1 Cor. 10:24, 33).

The Deaconship. Let's take a closer look at the word *deacon* (servant) in the New Testament. The word *deacon* can be applied in two ways. First, it can be applied to all Christians who are called to serve Jesus Christ and His people. This is seen in the broad-based ministry of household servants.

THE HEART ALL LEADERS MUST DEVELOP

Second, it can be applied to the official appointment of certain deacons as representatives of the local church, and as set into that office by the local leadership (Acts 6:1-4). Stephen and Philip were two appointed deacons (Acts 6:5—8:40). Both had powerful ministries, which should forever stamp into our minds that the office of deacon was never intended by God to be a despised or weak office in the New Testament Church.

If you are a Christian, whether or not you have been appointed as a deacon, your ministry will profit from studying the principles of deaconship. The qualifications for deaconship are a part of the qualifications for all Christian leaders. And the ministry of deaconship is the foundation of all congregational ministries.

The early Church believed that an official capacity of serving the people of God was very important. The Church outlined certain qualifications for deacons and their wives (1 Tim. 3:8-14), and appointed people to the office (Phil. 1:1). Paul exhorted the deacons to use their office in the right way, implying that their office was invested with enough authority to create the possibility of improper use (1 Tim. 3:10, 13). Paul admonished the deacons to live up to the title of their office, that of "servant to God's people."

Three key words in New Testament Greek develop the idea of being a minister to God's people.

The word *diakoneo* (1 Tim. 3:10, 13) is a verb which means to be an attendant, to wait upon. It is usually used in a domestic setting, as the work of a household servant.

The word *diakonia* is a noun, which refers to the aid or service that a servant or official renders to someone else.

The word *diakonos* (Phil. 1:1; 1 Tim. 3:8, 12)

means to run errands, to attend on someone, or to do any menial task.

These three words describe all the primary elements of the deaconship: the act of service, the service itself, and the one who serves.

The New Testament writers borrowed the Greek word for deacon and developed it as a part of their vocabulary. Originally, the word referred to waiting on tables (as the deacons did in Acts 6:1-4). Later, it broadened to include the idea of providing or caring for any need of another person. Even later, the word was used to refer to the service or act of showing love to another person in a personal way, as from one friend to another. All of these meanings applied to every Christian in the house of God.

To the Jews, however, the idea of menial service was abhorrent. May the Lord deliver us from such attitudes and give us true servants' hearts.

The following material on deaconship is in general outline form, to help the reader study this subject in greater detail.

Diakoneo. The following scriptures use the word *diakoneo*, and show different examples of the "act of serving" in the early Church. Each of these scriptures can be applied in principle to the duties of service required of every Christian in the Body of Christ.

After being healed of sickness, Peter's mother-in-law "arose and ministered unto" Jesus and the disciples (Matt. 8:15).

On the Day of Judgment, said Jesus, service to the needy would be likened to service to Christ Himself. "'Lord, when saw we thee an hungered, or athirst, or a stranger, or naked, or sick, or in prison, and did not minister unto thee?'. . . .'Inasmuch as ye did it not to one of the least of these, ye did it not to me'" (Matt. 25:44, 45).

"But now I go unto Jerusalem to minister unto

the saints," said the apostle Paul (Rom. 15:25). He knew it might well lead to his death.

"As every man hath received the gift, even so minister the same one to another, as good stewards of the manifold grace of God. . . . if any man minister, let him do it as of the ability which God giveth," said the apostle Peter (1 Pet. 4:10, 11b). This last verse from the apostle Peter clearly establishes that all Christians are called and empowered to serve (minister).

Diakonia. The following scriptures use the word *diakonia* (which along with *diakoneo* occurs 70 times in the New Testament), showing us "the service of ministry" and establishing the office of the deacon.

In Acts 1:24-25, the apostles asked God to "show whether of these two (Joseph or Matthias) thou hast chosen, that he may take part of this ministry and apostleship, from which Judas by transgression fell."

The apostle Paul admonishes Archippus to "take heed to the ministry which thou hast received in the Lord" (Col. 4:17).

From prison, Paul asks his disciple Timothy to bring Mark to him on Timothy's next visit, "For he is profitable to me for the ministry" (2 Tim. 4:11).

In Revelation, the message to the church in Thyatira was, "I know thy works, and charity, and service, and faith" (Rev. 2:19).

Diakonos. As a description of one who serves, the Greek word *diakonos* appears 30 times in the New Testament. It comes from the word *diako*, to run errands. It is translated with three English words: minister, servant, and deacon. From its use, it is apparent that not only those who are officially designated as "deacons" are to serve others, but that all Christians are to serve. For further study, the list of verses where *diakonos* appears is:

MINISTER	SERVANTS
Matt. 20:26	Matt. 23:11
Mark 10:43	Matt. 22:13
Rom. 13:4	Mark 9:35
Rom. 15:8	John 2:5
1 Cor. 3:5	John 2:9
Eph. 3:7	John 12:26
Col. 1:25	Rom. 16:1
1 Thess. 3:2	
2 Cor. 3:6	DEACONS
2 Cor. 6:4	Phil. 1:1
2 Cor. 11:15	1 Tim. 3:8
2 Cor. 11:23	1 Tim. 3:12
Gal. 2:17	
Col. 1:7	
Col. 1:23	
Col. 4:7	
1 Tim. 4:6	

Particular Forms of Ministry. Service is coupled with other words to describe a particular form of ministry.

The "ministry of the word" (2 Tim. 4:5) reminds us that a preacher is one who serves up the bread of life (Acts 6:4).

We hear of "the ministry of reconciliation" in 2 Corinthians 5:18.

Self-effort to keep all the requirements of the law is called "the ministry of death and condemnation," but the life of faith is a "ministry of the spirit and a ministry of righteousness" (2 Cor. 3:7-9).

Several verses use diakonos to show that people can be servants of many things. It is possible to be a servant of Satan (2 Cor. 11:14-15). God wants us to be, instead, servants of God (2 Cor. 6:3), of Christ (1 Tim. 4:6), of the Gospel (2 Cor. 11:23), of the new Covenant (2 Cor. 3:6), and of the Church (Col. 1:25). God desires us, as servants, to perform any task that the Spirit tells us to do, whether it appears menial or important.

Examples of Servants

Leaders can sometimes become isolated. They may think they are the only ones trying to fulfill the ministry of service to God, Christ, the Gospel, the New Covenant, and the Church. Fortunately, this is wrong. The New Testament presents an inspiring list of individuals and groups who were and are called to serve God and the Church in their own particular ways.

Timothy and Erastus (Acts 19:22; *diakonos*, 1 Tim. 3:2 and 4:6)

Onisiphorus' service to Paul at Ephesus (2 Tim. 1:16-18)

Apostles' service to the Church (2 Cor. 3:3)

Old Testament prophets to the Church (1 Pet. 1:10-12)

Paul ministering to needs of the saints at Jerusalem (2 Cor. 8:19; Rom. 15:31)

Ministry of saints in general (Eph. 4:11; Heb. 6:10)

Household of Stephen devoting themselves to the service of the saints (1 Cor. 16:15)

Ministry of angels (Heb. 1:14; Mark 1:13)

Archippus (Col. 4:17)

Tychicus (Eph. 6:21; Col. 4:7, *diakonos*)

Epaphras (Col. 1:7, *diakonos*)

The Lord Jesus Christ provides us the best example of servanthood. In His earthly ministry among the Jews, He totally overturned their negative attitudes toward servanthood by becoming a servant in every way. He served from His birth to His death. The Church must make sure that she does not stumble over the requirement to serve, but instead she must follow the example of her Master

Servant, Jesus Christ. Let's explore the teaching and life example of Christ the servant in the following verses:

Luke 12:37: The Lord will reward men and women who keep a constant watch for opportunities to serve Him, by serving them Himself: "He shall gird himself, and make them to sit down to meat, and will come forth and serve them."

Luke 22:27: "Which is greater, one who sits at the table or one who serves? I am among you as one who serves."

John 13: In this chapter, Jesus takes the place of a slave, and washes the disciples' feet.

Mark 10:43: "Not lording it over them . . . whosoever will be great let him be your servant. The first must be a slave."

John 12:24-26: If anyone serves me, he must follow me, and where I am, there shall be my servant. Also . . . if anyone serves me, the Father will honor him."

Phil. 2:8: "Jesus took the form of a servant and humbled Himself unto the death on the cross." Jesus had bound Himself to be God's servant, and accepted the full measure of labor and suffering required to complete His service.

In all of these verses (with the exception of John 13, where the example of Jesus says all), some form of the word *diakonos* is employed for "servant." May every leader develop a servant's heart like Christ's.

Part 4

THE HEART OF A SHEPHERD

*A*s we study the shepherd's heart, you may see Jehovah and the Lord Jesus Christ in new ways. That's because the heart of a shepherd is the heart of the Lord for His Church.

A shepherd's heart is a required attitude in all leadership ministries. What better way to be a Christian, a "Christ-like one," than to love the Church as Christ loves her? If you want to understand Christian leadership, if you want to know Christ, you'll want to study what the Bible has to say about the heart of a shepherd.

"Shepherd" as a Leadership Title

God's leaders are given many titles in both the Old Testament and the New Testament. Some of these titles are bishop, presbyter, priest, preacher, minister, and shepherd. Each word has a history and significance of its own. But the term *shepherd* has a particular importance to God.

Interestingly, the word *shepherd* has probably seen the least use of all these titles throughout Church history. Such infrequent use of the word shows that many of the leaders of the Church have not fully experienced or practiced true shepherding. Let's survey each of the titles above, and see how they all fall short of truly representing God's idea of the shepherd-servant.

Bishop. The word *bishop* came into the Church

THE HEART ALL LEADERS MUST DEVELOP

from the Gentile world. It is used to designate a leader who oversees or superintends the flock of God. In the Apostolic era, all local churches had bishops. Since the word directly calls up images of authority and administration, however, many Church leaders have abused this title for dictatorial ends. Even in its original form, bishop does not completely describe the meaning that God invested in the word *shepherd*.

Presbyter The word *presbyter* came into the Church from Judaism. As far back as the time of Moses, Jews had this kind of leader. The New Testament uses *bishop* and *presbyter* interchangeably, even as the early Church combined the Gentile and the Jewish worlds. In the early Church, presbyters (elders) were primarily men of some years. The word *presbyter* is based on age and experience, which does not take in the full scope of the meaning in shepherd.

Priest. The word *priest* has a long history in both Judaism and paganism. In Judaism, the priest represented the people to their God, and God to His people. Jesus and His disciples used this word very little in the New Testament. The ultimate New Testament meaning of priest, as it applies to individual Christians, was given to Peter. Peter called the Church "a royal priesthood" (1 Peter 2:5, 9). But since the office of priesthood involves the work of representing and mediating, it misses the important element of guidance that shepherd contains. The term *priest* has been one of the most abused terms when applied to Christian leadership, producing spiritual bondage for many people—a far cry from the intent of the shepherd.

Preacher. The word *preacher* has a great tradition in the Church of describing the public speaking aspect of the shepherd (pastor). The meaning and high value placed on this title has led, unfortunately, to the false belief that success as an orator equates with success in shepherding the flock. But since the concept of preaching depends heavily on a pulpit/pew kind of relationship, it is very far from the process of shepherding.

Minister. The word *minister* has been applied to Church leaders (particularly pastors), whether the leaders are professionally ordained by man or spiritually ordained by God. Our applications of the word sometimes give no distinction between a true servant of God and a man who falsely dons the same title. Even if a man is not divinely called, even if he is neither willing nor able to serve God's people, he can be ordained and called a minister by the state government.

An unfortunate attitude rising from the Church's misuse of the term *minister* is that only the one man called *minister* is the servant of God. Instead, God calls each Christian to a particular ministry function. This confusion over the definition of *minister* has led to the idea that only an ordained minister is competent to do the spiritual work of the Church. Thus the word *minister* has been given an idea of professionalism which clashes with the true meaning of shepherd.

Shepherd. Finally, we have the beautifully descriptive title of *shepherd*. Throughout her history, the Church has probably used this title of ministry least, because it represents the ministerial function most lacking in the Church. At times, the Church has obviously lacked the true ministerial function of the shepherd: tender, sincere, intimate, loving, spiritual care of a shepherd for his flock. Fortunately, God is again greatly emphasizing this most significant title of ministry.

Everyone who wants to fulfill his or her area of responsibility in the kingdom of God must have the heart qualifications of a leader. He needs the heart of the father to nurture the people of the Lord to maturity. She needs the heart of the servant to sacrifice time and life to minister to every need of God's people. Now we come to the heart attitude of the shepherd. Everyone involved in the work of the Lord must have a shepherd's heart—it's not just for the "full-time" minister.

Periodically, the Church passes through seasons of great need for true shepherds. When Church leadership is immature or failing, the sheep are scattered, wounded, and bruised just as were the children of God in different times during Israel's history.

Numbers 27:15-17: When Moses' leadership of Israel was ending, he asked the Lord to "set a man over the congregation . . . that the congregation of the Lord be not as sheep which have no shepherd."

1 Kings 22:17: When the prophet Micaiah prophesied a military defeat at the hands of Syria: "I

saw all Israel scattered upon the hills, as sheep that have not a shepherd."

Ezekiel 34:4-6: "My flock became meat to every beast of the field, because there was no (true) shepherd. . . . I will deliver my flock from their mouth (of false shepherds), that they may not be meat for them."

Zechariah 10:2: "They were troubled because there was no shepherd."

Zechariah 13:7: "Smite the shepherd and the sheep will be scattered" is a prophecy of Christ's death.

Jehovah as the Great Shepherd

A shepherd is "a man who takes care of the sheep, a person who cares for and protects the sheep; a spiritual guide, friend, or companion." This describes a natural shepherd's work of protecting, guiding, and feeding the flock. A spiritual shepherd does the same spiritual work of protecting, guiding, and feeding God's people. The Lord is called a shepherd of His people many times throughout Scripture. He is our example, the source of the true definition of what He wants us to be and do as shepherds. He is the Great Shepherd of our souls:

Ps. 23:1: "The Lord is my shepherd."

Ps. 80:1: "Give ear, O shepherd of Israel."

Ezek. 34:12: "I will search for my sheep as a shepherd does a flock."

Isa. 40:11: "He shall feed his flock like a shepherd."

Ps. 77:20: "Thou leadest thy people like a flock.

Actions of the Great Shepherd

The Lord of the Old Testament is the Great Shepherd to His flock Israel, and more. He also illustrates, to all spiritual shepherds throughout all ages, the proper attitudes and actions of a shepherd of God's people. The list below names some of the actions that arose from the shepherd's heart of the Lord in the Old Testament.

Ezek. 34:11-16

Searched out the lost sheep

Ezek. 34:12

Delivered the captive sheep

Ezek. 34:13

Gathered the dispersed sheep

Isa. 40:11, Ezek. 34:13

Fed the hungry sheep

Ps. 23:1-3, Ezek. 34:15

Rested the weary sheep

Ezek. 34:16

Bound up the hurt sheep

Ezek. 34:16

Strengthened the weak sheep

Ps. 23:3

Guided the directionless sheep

Isa. 40:11

Carried the broken sheep

Ps. 23:3

Restored the soul of the tired sheep

Ps. 23:4

Comforted the agitated sheep

Ps. 23:5

Prepared a table for the frightened sheep

Ps. 23:5

Anointed the needy sheep

Jesus as the Good Shepherd

In the New Testament, we find the revelation of God in the flesh, the Lord Jesus Christ, as the Good Shepherd of the sheep. Jesus displays all of the attributes of God's shepherding heart. As we see His life unfold in the New Testament gospels, we see the heart of Jehovah made manifest. Jesus Christ was the good shepherd of His sheep in the Gospels as Jehovah was the Great Shepherd of Israel in the Old Testament. The following scriptures show Jesus as the Good Shepherd of the New Testament:

John 10:11, 14	"I am the good shepherd"
Heb. 13:20	"Jesus, the great shepherd of the sheep"
1 Pet. 2:25	"Return unto the shepherd and bishop of your souls"
1 Pet. 5:4	"When the chief shepherd shall appear"

As we listed the heart attitudes of the Lord in the Old Testament, so we list the heart attitudes and actions of Jesus Christ, the pattern Shepherd in the New Testament. Most of these insights are derived from John 10.

Jesus:

Matt. 9:35, 36; John 10:15b	Cares for the sheep.
John 10:3	Relates to the sheep.
John 10:1	Condemns all who reject the Door of the sheepfold, and enter some other way, as thieves and robbers
John 10:8	Condemns all who came before Him as thieves and robbers.
John 10:1	Provides a sheepfold for the sheep.
John 10:3, 4	Leads the sheep.
John 10:2	Enters by the Door Himself.
John 10:3a	Has the doorkeeper open to Him.
John 10:6	Provides spiritual insight for the sheep.

John 10:3b, 27a	Makes His voice plain to His sheep.
John 10:3c	Calls His own sheep by name.
John 10:3d	Leads His own sheep out into pasture.
John 10:4a, b	Goes before His own sheep as He leads them out.
John 10:4c, 27c	Has the sheep follow Him.
John 10:4d	Has the sheep recognize His voice.
John 10:7, 9a	Is the Door of the sheep.
John 10:9	Feeds the sheep.
John 10:10b	Gives life to the sheep by protecting them.
John 10:10b, 11b, 15c, 17	Gives His life for the sheep.
John 10:11a, 14a	Is the Good Shepherd of the sheep.

John 10:12a, 13a	Is a true shepherd of His sheep and the opposite of a hireling.
John 10:12c	Is the owner of the sheep and not a hireling.
John 10:12d	Sees when the wolf comes to destroy the flock.
John 10:12e,f	Stays near the sheep when the wolf comes, in contrast to the cowardly hireling.
John 10:14b, 27b	Knows His own sheep.
John 10:14c	Is known by His own sheep
John 10:15b	Knows the Father.
John 10:15a	Is known by the Father.
John 10:16a	Has other sheep in other folds.
John 10:16c	Brings in the other sheep also.

John 10:16d	Is heard by the other sheep as well.
John 10:16e	Is the One Shepherd and owner of all folds.
John 10:17c	Takes up His life again because He laid it down.
John 10:18abc	Lays His life down freely and of His own initiative.
John 10:18d	Has the authority to lay down His life because God Himself has commissioned Him to do so.

The Lord Jesus showed us the attitude and actions of a true shepherd throughout His entire ministry. He set forth an example for all the shepherds of God's flock. Jesus was a man of compassion and love. He did not rely on crowds and multitudes of followers to measure his success in shepherding. On the contrary, He looked for the sheep with needs, and He identified those needs. Then He was not satisfied until He met the individual needs of each sheep.

Today, how do the shepherds of the Church see the people of the Lord? Do our shepherds see the people of God as a crowd of sheep, hungry for rich food and entertainment? Or do they see them as broken people in great need of love and compassion? Today, unfortunately, the majority of Church leaders are not doing the work of a true shepherd. The Church desperately needs true shepherds, who will lay down their lives for the sheep, as Jesus did. The Church needs spiritual shepherds to heal the broken-hearted and bind up the wounds of the hurt. The contemporary Church has enough theologians who love to write or verbalize the knowledge of God. She needs shepherds who have true spiritual ministries to God's people.

Relational Pictures of a Leader

In short, the Church needs leaders who themselves have an intimate relationship with God, and who can bring others into the same communion with God. The Bible uses many different pictures (described below) to demonstrate this need for relationship—pictures that can guide spiritual shepherds in relationships with their sheep.

Father and Child Relationship. This is a picture of the warm, loving relationship between a father and his children. In this relationship the children love and respect the father, and respond to his corrective hand. Here we see the shepherd, like the father, whose primary purpose is to cause his children sincerely and without fear to love him, their mother, their brothers and sisters, and those outside of the family. Fathers also seek to mature their children in all of their relationships in life.

Husband and Wife Relationship. This is a picture

of the love relationship of Christ with His Church, the bond of marriage with all its sacred meaning. The husband provides the home and supports his wife in love. The wife receives and responds to his love. Here we see how the shepherd must be the initiator in giving his love to his sheep, and how he must provide them with a good spiritual home.

Head and Body Relationship. This is a picture of a relationship of governing and protecting. Just as Christ governs and protects His Church, which is His Body, so the shepherd must take his rod and staff in hand and govern and protect his local church body. In both of these pictures, the head is the covering for the body. The body is many-membered, but the head is singular. As a body has only one head, the shepherd must remember that Christ continues as the only Head of the body. The undershepherd takes up his leadership responsibility in service and support of the Head, Christ.

Vine and Branches Relationship. The Lord Jesus presents this picture of a relationship between Himself and the Church in John 15. In these verses, He is the vine and His people are the branches. All of the life, source, and power for the branches must come from the vine. There is such a close relationship between the vine and the branches that one cannot always discern where the vine ends and the branches begin. Jesus said the branches must bear fruit, or they will be purged by the husbandman. If need be, the husbandman will take his sharp knife and cut away the worthless parts of a branch. So it is with the shepherd, who should develop such a close relationship with his sheep that they will allow him to sheer away some of the unprofitable areas of their lives.

Husbandman and Vineyard Relationship. This is the picture of a vineyard meticulously cared for by a husbandman or farmer. At times, the vineyard is overgrown, and so the husbandman must come and clean out all the debris. At times he must skillfully use his tools to harvest the vineyard's fruit. Similarly, God's shepherds must be sensitive enough to his sheep that he can discern the spiritual times and seasons in their lives.

Potter and Clay Relationship. This is a picture of the hand of God which forms His vessel, the Church. The potter's hand is in complete control of the clay. The clay cannot ask the potter what he is doing. This is the way the Lord deals with His people. Similarly, the shepherd should be able to so relate to his sheep that he can help form Christ's character in their lives.

Captain and Army Relationship. The picture here is one of discipline and authority. The army of the Lord is a place of correction and training. The army must experience many drills in order to be useful to its captain in warfare. At this time, the Church is under the hand of the mighty Son of David, the Captain of her salvation, Jesus Christ. Similarly, the shepherd must train and discipline his sheep to fit them for their tasks.

Creator and Creature Relationship. God is the all-powerful Creator whose words brought into being the worlds. At His word, all that is in the heavens and earth was formed. This is a picture of the mighty God reproducing His own image and likeness in His creation. The relationship here is not a very personal one, because man alienated himself from God through disobedience. Through obedience, however, man can enter again into a relationship with his Creator. Similarly, the shepherd should be the instrument through which God can create new life in His people.

Shepherd and Sheep Relationship. This last picture of the shepherd and the sheep is a picture of warmth and beauty. Love, compassion, and tenderness are exchanged. This is demonstrated in the shepherd carrying his small, hurt lamb upon his shoulders to safety. Since this illustration is also shown in one of the titles of God (The Great Shepherd), it holds a tender picture of true ministry.

The Shepherd-Watchman

The requirements for a natural shepherd apply directly to the spiritual shepherds of God's people. Natural shepherds, as watchmen over their flock, build observation towers to scan the countryside for advance warning of dangers to the flock. Flash floods can sweep through the hills and destroy everything in their path. Predators may raid the flock; lions, bears, jackals, or wolves could sneak in and claim a straying lamb or wounded sheep. These predators, in fact, are a threat to the shepherd himself. Vultures or eagles might swoop down to wound the young of the flock, and return later for the kill. The shepherd must be a far-seeing watchman, constantly alert to potential dangers around him and the flock. He dare not be a lazy or unseeing watchman.

Paul exhorted the Ephesian elders, in his farewell address, to watch over the flock in just this way (Acts 20:28-31). Paul's letter to the Corinthians exhorts them to watch and stand fast (1 Cor. 16:13). Other examples of the call to shepherdly watchfulness:

"Watch ye and stand fast" (1 Cor. 16:13).

"Continue in prayer and watch" (Col. 4:2).

"Let us not sleep, but let us watch" (1 Thess. 5:6).

"But watch thou in all things" (2 Tim. 4:5).

"Obey them who have rule over you. . . . for they watch for your souls" (Heb. 13:17).

A leader over the flock must be a most diligent watchman. The Church has many enemies that would attack the house of the Lord in these last days. Lazy shepherds leave the Church open to attack. And false shepherds have inflicted some of the Church's worst wounds. Not only do they steal from God's people, but they often bring forth a response of misguided over-regulation from government. True and watchful shepherds of spiritual Israel are the Church's hope of protection from spiritual destruction in these perilous times.

The Shepherd-Protector

Closely related to the role of watchman is the shepherd's role as guard, protector, and defender of the flock. Sheep are among the most defenseless of animals. They have no natural weapons for attack. Their docile disposition leaves them very unlikely to bite, kick, or scratch. They are one of the only animals that depend almost completely on a human protector. The shepherd is the flock's main (if not the only) guard and protector against hazards and enemies. At times, the shepherd must risk his own life for the life of the sheep.

Sheep are also very ignorant about personal survival in the wilderness. The shepherd must exercise constant watch over the sheep in the wilderness, where they invariably wander into trouble. In the wilderness, shepherds used to build a sheepfold with walls that could repel the strongest predators. Shepherds slept by the door to provide complete security for the flock. If an enemy came first, he would have to step over the shepherd to get to the sheep.

The Lord, the Great Shepherd of the sheep, gives us His standard and his example of how to defend the flock. In Psalms 121:3, we are assured that "He that keepeth thee will not slumber." Other verses that give us the Lord's standard and example for His under-shepherds in being a true defender of the flock:

Ps. 7:10	"My defense is of God."
Ps. 59:16	"Thou hast been my defense and my refuge."
Ps. 62:6	"He is my defense; I shall not be moved."
Zech. 9:15	"The Lord of Hosts shall defend them."
Ps. 121:3	"He that keepeth thee shall not slumber."
Ps. 12:7	"Thou shall keep them, O Lord."
Ps. 31:20	"The Lord shall keep them safely in his pavilion."
Ps. 127:1	"Except the Lord keep the city."
John 17:11	"Holy Father, keep them through thy own word."

The Lord Jesus is the Great Shepherd who shall keep His people from all trouble. In the same way, each of His shepherd-leaders must do all he can to protect the sheep from their enemies.

The Shepherd-Guide

A shepherd must perform another important role for the sheep—that of guide. To say the least, sheep are not independent travelers. They have no sense of direction. Astray from the flock, they wander in circles until taken by predators. When grazing, they keep their noses to the ground as long as there is grass, but never look up to see where their grazing takes them.

Conditions in the wilderness are not kind to sheep. Good pasture is often in spots and small strips, and is hard to find. Streams may be few in number and hidden in some areas, making the land parched and unyielding. Without a shepherd, sheep would wander aimlessly until they died of starvation or thirst. The shepherd must wisely select grazing range for the sheep, out of personal, first-hand knowledge. The lives of the sheep depend on his guidance.

Sheep are sensitive animals that cannot endure hard driving. They are meant to be led gently, and the wise shepherd does so. Some weak, sickly, or injured sheep would die if the shepherd drove them too far or too fast. The wisdom of the shepherd can save the lives of many sheep. The patriarch Jacob illustrates this truth. In Genesis 33:9-15, we have the account of Jacob guiding his flock as he went back to his home country. He demonstrated many important attitudes as a shepherd over his flock.

Tenderness – Gen. 33:13: "The children are tender."

Sensitivity – Gen. 33:13: "The flocks and the herds have young with them."

Gentleness – Gen. 33:13: "The flock will die if men overdrive them in one day."

Watchfulness – Gen. 33:14: "The flock must be led softly."

Patience – Gen. 33:14: "The flock must only be

lead as much as the youngest can endure."

These verses in Genesis 33 clearly show the heart of a true shepherd. Jacob was willing to go slowly in order to save the young and the tender of the flock. He did not drive the flock, though he had the power to do so and it would have had its benefits. Similarly, the Church of the Lord Jesus has many young and tender sheep. These cannot be driven hard by forceful men. They must be gently guided by true shepherds.

God has promised to help His shepherds guide the flock effectively. He will be their Great shepherd, the One whose example and guidance the under-shepherd can follow.

Promises for the shepherd:

Ps. 23:2	"He leadeth me beside the still waters."
Ps. 77:20	"Thou leadest thy people like a flock."

Ps. 78:52, 54   "He led forth his own
                   sheep and guided them
                   in the wilderness like a
                   flock."

The Shepherd-Physician

The shepherd must also be a physician to his sheep. The English word *physician* means a person who heals, relieves, or comforts. In the Hebrew language, the concept of physician is one who mends by stitching, cures, causes healing, repairs, and makes whole. In the Greek language, the concept means to make whole and to set free by curing.

These various definitions capture the shepherd's ministry. The spiritual shepherd is to heal the broken-hearted and mend the torn. This is the true work of those who have a shepherd's heart. Like people, sheep may suffer from a variety of maladies and diseases. Consequently, they need shepherds who are competent as physicians. The spiritual shepherd must have spiritual discernment regarding the problems that can overtake his flock. He must correctly diagnose and treat these sicknesses, or they may prove fatal to the sheep.

Jesus showed His concern for the hurting sheep of Israel when He visited the "publicans and sinners." To the Pharisees who objected to this, He replied, "They that be whole need not a physician, but they who are sick" (Matt. 9:12).

Many sick people in the Church today need a shepherd-physician. They suffer in any number of ways—emotionally, spiritually, mentally, physically. It takes a true spiritual physician to heal God's flock, not an over-intellectual academic. The ability to cooperate with the Holy Spirit in the healing of souls requires experience in the school of the spirit, and a knowledge of the Word of God's practical application to everyday life.

Job rejected would-be physicians who attempted to meet his needs through inadequate human understanding and knowledge. "Ye are all physicians of no value," he said (Job 13:4). We must ask ourselves, "How many shepherds are in this same category?" Unfortunately, too many "ministers" are of little value to the flock of God, because they cannot discern the spiritual needs of the sheep.

What practical value does a shepherd have, without the ability to meet the practical needs of hurting sheep? Preaching well does not negate the need for shepherd-physicians. Without an understanding of the main purpose of a shepherd's work, understanding all of the brilliant professors of the past and the knowledge of many languages have no value. The sheep need shepherds who can stitch up the wounded and bind up the brokenhearted. The need today is for God-anointed shepherds with skill and wisdom as spiritual physicians, who can diagnose and treat the sheep of God.

Like other creatures, sheep have unforeseen accidents and misfortunes. They may break their legs, get cut, fall into pits, or bruise themselves. At different seasons, they are prone to different diseases or conditions. Different environments and different food affect sheep in different ways. Sickness can overtake a sheep even if it does nothing wrong. The shepherd must not always blame the sheep for their suffering; he must guard his attitude toward the sheep and not become hardened to their cries.

Sensitivity to the sheep is a must for the shepherd's work of ministry. A shepherd must not beat a sheep for falling into a hole or punish a sheep for getting bruised in a thicket. Our Chief Shepherd, the Lord Jesus, never showed a hastiness to condemn the sheep. A true shepherd feels the hurt of the sheep and suffers a sheep's bruises as if they were his own. A shepherd accepts the problems of the sheep. They will fall into pits and holes. They will catch colds and need special attention. It is the responsibility and the very life of the shepherd to meet such needs. If all the sheep were well, there would be less need for the shepherd's ministry. The sheep that are sick need a physician, not the ones that are whole.

Some shepherds want a flock that is healthy and without needs. This is virtually impossible. The true shepherd, on the other hand, is always looking for sheep with needs. He looks for a broken leg, a bruised heel, a cut foot, a bad eating habit. The true shepherd finds his very fulfillment in tending the needs of the sheep! The spiritual shepherd should always remember that a needy sheep that limps from a foot wound or does not feed due to an infirmity should receive more abundant care and attention. God's Church is not a business, with a "spiritual sales quota" on every "employee." The

Body of Christ is the flock of the Great Shepherd. The shepherd is called by God to heal the broken-hearted, not to condemn those who need his help.

Sheep Diseases

The shepherd must watch over his flock, alert for signs of common sheep diseases and maladies. The following list of sheep diseases can also serve as a warning list to God's spiritual shepherds. It will explore how each of these diseases is analogous to a spiritual disease or problem that can occur in the Church.

Natural Disease: Overeating Disease

（may come from）

- A sudden change of food
- An excess of high energy food
- Irregular feeding times
- Increasing amount of food too rapidly

- Feeding lambs of varying sizes together

Spiritual Application

- A sudden change of teaching or spiritual food of any kind can be fatal to many people; change must come slowly and progressively.

- To give the people a rich, potent teaching diet continually is to spiritually overfeed them. A variety of teaching and preaching is needed.

- To upset regular feeding times does harm to the people. They need a definite feeding time to be consistently satisfied.

- To increase the amount of ministry, teaching, or preaching too quickly will harm the people. The spiritual shepherd must discern the people's growth level and meet them where they are.

- All people do not have the same spiritual need. The flock has different levels of growth and maturity. Each different level of the people requires a specialized ministry.

Natural Disease: White Muscle Disease

(may come from)

- Vitamin deficiency

- Imbalanced diet

- Death of offspring (result)

Spiritual Application

- The people must be kept on a straight, nutritional diet of the Word of God exclusively.

- The people must have a balanced diet of practical, devotional, spiritual, inspirational, and instructional food for proper growth.

- Spiritual reproduction of the people will be stifled if their diet is imbalanced.

Natural Disease: Twin Lamb Disease

(may come from)

- Low blood pressure due to stress

- The ewes with a tendency toward this disease can be discovered when the shepherd even gently drives the sheep, and they show no energy to be driven.

Spiritual Application

• Undue pressure upon the sheep may cause ill spiritual births.

• The most productive members of the flock need close attention, including a double portion of food and energy.

Natural Disease: Grass Tetany Disease

(may come from)

• Low magnesium in the blood, due to lush grass

• Not enough variety in the food

Spiritual Application

• A mixture of lush spiritual food with dry food is needed when the sheep are fed with the Word. Too much of the same kind of teaching or preaching will cause illness in the people.

Natural Disease: Pneumonia

(may come from)

• Excessive stress on the sheep

Spiritual Application

• The shepherd must not be guilty of oppressing the flock. The shepherd must not overdrive those under his authority.

Natural Disease: Foot Rot Disease

(may come from)

• Too much time in wet pasture

• Threatens the mobility of the sheep

Spiritual Application

• Dry spiritual periods are needed, as well as wet periods, as the people are washed in the water of the Word and follow the Spirit on a daily basis. Excessive watering with the Word, without balance, cripples the walk of the people.

Natural Disease: Bloat Disease

(may come from)

• Feeding on lush legumes and pastures, which disturbs the sheeps' digestion

Spiritual Application

• Too much rich teaching that cannot be put into action causes problems in the life of the people and will result in immediate spiritual death.

Natural Disease: Parasitic Disease

• Parasites may attach either to external or internal parts of a sheep's body

• Unhealthiness in the walk of the sheep

Spiritual Application

• The shepherd must at times inspect the people for hidden areas that will bring spiritual death. He must also be aware of the outward involvements that may be sapping all of the strength out of the people's relationships with God.

• If this problem goes unchecked, it will weaken the lives of the people and their dedication to the Lord and His work.

Natural Disease: Poisonous Plants Diseases

• Poisonous plants are usually hidden among nutritional plants

• Sheep generally do not know the difference between poisonous and nutritional plants

Spiritual Application

• The shepherd must carefully examine all the sources from which his people receive their teaching and preaching.

• The people must learn to recognize the difference between good and bad teaching through the teaching of their shepherd.

Types of Sheep

The shepherd-physician should be aware of the

different kinds of sheep in his flock. Different sheep are prone to different problems. We will look at three different sheep "personalities" that have applications in spiritual truth for the spiritual shepherd.

Solitary sheep. This sheep constantly strays from the flock, and it does not eat with the flock. He is the loner of the flock. The shepherd may not notice his straying unless he identifies the sheep each time it strays. In spiritual analogy, this sheep has some real inward problems. He may have suffered deep emotional wounds, causing a lack of trust in the other sheep or in the shepherd. The solitary sheep might feel the other sheep are too mature or immature for his fellowship. All three of these attitudes are unhealthy and need the shepherd's help and correction.

Fear of exposure is common among solitary sheep. The exposure of past sins, habits, or hurts keeps this sheep from healthy fellowship. Some

solitary sheep, on the other hand, are merely looking for attention. They will do anything, even sepa-
rate themselves, to be noticed and attended by the
shepherd or other sheep. Such an attention-seeker
needs immediate help, because avoiding fellowship
can cause many serious problems.

Hermit sheep. Though similar to the solitary
sheep in some ways, the hermit sheep avoids the
flock for different reasons. The hermit sheep stays
away from the flock to avoid being sheared or
clipped by the shepherd. It has an uncanny way of
knowing when shearing time is approaching. It will
do anything to avoid the clipping process.

The shepherd must continuously watch for the
hermit sheep so it cannot hide. The uncut wool of
the hermit sheep will eventually grow long enough
to cover his eyes and blind him. In this condition,
he will surely run into serious problems. Predators,
thickets, and pits are just a few of the dangers he

can no longer avoid. His unclipped wool becomes heavy enough to slow him down, making him fall behind the flock to become an easy target for predators. When the flock is moved to better pasture, the hermit sheep is left behind so that he does not influence the other sheep.

God intends for all of His people to bear fruit. In the analogy of the hermit sheep, we see a Christian who wants to keep all the blessings and fruit in his life for his own enjoyment. Money is one example. But time, talents, relationship, and service to the Church are all areas where a spiritual hermit sheep needs to give. God's economy is not like the world's economy, where scarcity rules and storing up blessings is the natural response. In God's economy, His people must be givers, and more will be given to them. Though we give with the intention to bless God and bless others, it is also true that we receive more when we are giving more.

Wandering sheep. He is among the most dangerous of all. To the wandering sheep, the grass is always greener somewhere else, so he's always looking for a way out of the sheepfold or pasture. He spends all of his time looking for escape, and he usually finds an opening in the fence, a hole in the ground, or a gate left open.

The wandering sheep never settles down to enjoy the present pasture, and he breeds discontent among the other sheep as well. Because his bad influence especially affects the young of the flock, he is removed from the flock. In the Church, that wandering spirit must be broken and harnessed to a healthy purpose. The shepherd must accomplish this before the wandering sheep destroys himself, and many others.

These three types of sheep are only examples of the many problem personalities that the spiritual shepherd should know. He must discern the needs and problems in his sheep, and learn how to minister to them effectively.

Hireling vs. Shepherd

The opposite of a true shepherd is a hireling. Inherent in the word hireling is the essence of its meaning: "One who is hired for wages by day or by year." Technically, most people fit in that category today. Most people are paid to work for a set time period. To express the difference in today's terms, the difference between a hireling and a shepherd is like the difference between someone who has only a job (no matter how important the position) and someone who has a healthy career.

The person who has only a job assigns a dollar value to the mere passing of time. He may even cheat his employer in any number of ways to increase his "earnings." The person with a healthy career values all of his work relationships and tries to increase his productivity in order to build a better future.

Even that comparison, however, fails to capture the great contrast the Old Testament makes between the concepts of hireling and shepherd. The concept of a hireling is applied in the Old Testament to the following areas:

Ordinary laborers (1 Sam. 2:5; 2 Chron. 24:12)

Mercenary soldiers (2 Sam. 10:6; 2 Kings 7:6; 1 Chron. 19:6)

Goldsmiths (Isa. 46:6)

Bands of loose fellows (Judg. 9:4)

False priests (Judg. 18:4)

Balaam (Deut.23:4; Neh.13:2)

Hostile counselors (Ezra 4:5)

False prophets (Neh. 6:12)

In contrasting the general concept of a hireling with that of a shepherd, we could say that a hireling, as a leader, receives payment for his job but has no heart for it. A hireling is ambitious for position, power, and financial support, but he does not have a real love for God's people. A hireling certainly does not have a call of God or a shepherd's heart—the very existence of this attitude in his life is proof of that.

The following is a list of some of the obvious scriptural contrasts between a hireling and a shepherd.

Hireling vs. Shepherd

Hireling:

- Labors only for money (Matt. 20:7)
- Has no heart for the people
- Leaves when trouble comes (Jer. 46:21)
- Is unfaithful to his master

Shepherd:

- Labors out of love
- Has a heart for the people

- Gives his life for the sheep (John 10:11)
- Faithfully serves his master

Hireling:
- Feeds himself, and not the sheep (Ezek. 34:3)
- Neglects the sheep
- Lacks mercy (Ezek. 34:4)
- Is harsh, cruel, and forceful

Shepherd:
- Feeds the sheep
- Tenderly cares for the sheep
- Is full of mercy
- Is gentle, kind, and loving

Hireling:
- Drives the people too hard
- Scatters the sheep
- Is not willing to make personal sacrifices (Ezek. 34:2)

THE HEART ALL LEADERS MUST DEVELOP

- Is ambitious for position, but avoids responsibility

Shepherd:

- Leads the people wisely
- Unites the sheep
- Is always willing to make personal sacrifices
- Is not oriented to position, but has a servant's heart

Hireling:

- Does not take the time to bind up the sheep's wounds
- Dominates the sheep
- Does not care about the sheep's needs
- Produces unfruitfulness in the sheep

Shepherd:

- Binds the brokenhearted and heals the bruised
- Leads the sheep loving
- Discerns needs of the sheep
- Causes the sheep to be fruitful

Hireling:

- Is anxious at the close of day
- Has no part in the master's inheritance
- Makes no personal investment in the sheep
- Has no balance in discipline: too harsh, or not at all

Shepherd:

- Is peaceful and watchful (especially at night)
- Receives the flock of God as his inheritance
- Invests his life in the sheep, at the highest price he can pay
- Disciplines with the rod and the staff of God in love

Hireling:

- Limits his work to a given time period (Isa. 16:14; 21:16)
- Forgets the lost or those driven away
- Is a work of men's hands (see Ps. 135: 15-18; 115:4-8)

- Has a mouth that speaks not

Shepherd:

- Gives himself to his work full-time, because it is his calling and his lifestyle
- Seeks out the lost and those driven away
- Is a work of God's hands
- Has a mouth that speaks spiritual things

Hireling:

- Has eyes that see not
- Has ears that hear not
- Has a nose that senses not
- Has hands that do not touch or feel
- Produces his same unfeeling, undiscerning, and carnal nature in the people

Shepherd:

- Has eyes to discern spiritual things
- Has ears to hear spiritual things
- Has a nose to sense spiritual things
- Has hands that touch spiritual things

- Produces his same feeling, discerning, and spiritual nature in the people

May every spiritual shepherd forsake the way of the hireling and truly shepherd the flock of God.

Guard Your Heart

The heart of the shepherd is the closest thing to the heart of God for His Church. The Christian leader must do more than understand it—he or she must live it.

To its great loss, the leadership of the Church tends to follow leadership trends in society at large. During a time of economic expansion, the shepherds of God's sheep may adopt an "easy money, quick fix" attitude. They fail to build true spiritual strength in their churches, opting for a show of growth in new buildings, membership drives, and other outward displays of blessing.

Unfortunately, the heart condition of such leaders may erode a great deal further. During prosperous years, the drive to build and expand personal kingdoms in the Church goes on with a vengeance. In the middle of it all, some of the most successful Church leaders become some of the most carnal. They fail to guard their hearts. Their carnal sins may even grow more shocking than anything committed by their "peers" in society at large.

Our leaders must guard their hearts. Christian leaders are on the front line of the war with Satan. They must never forget that they can pass from the status of victor to the ranks of vanquished in a matter of moments. And when that happens, many in the Church will pass with them.

Even as a congregational ministry, you can exert a tremendous influence for good over the leaders of the Church. Your prayers are the daily defense that saves Christian leaders. It's quite likely that a lack of supporting prayer has been a major factor in the dissolution of some major ministries.

Have you ever watched the demise of a Christian leader, and said to yourself, "Now I realize that I saw it coming. There were signs of spiritual illness all along." Don't put your leaders on a pedestal and leave them there to die alone. Love them, pray for them, and correct them privately—before major problems develop—in a way that shows how much you support their ministries.

Let us all guard our hearts, and ask the Lord to develop in us His own heart, the heart of the shepherd.

Pursuing Heart Qualities

If you earnestly desire to know your spiritual calling, pursue the qualifications that make you the candidate to receive God's direction. Develop the generous heart of a father, the humble heart of a servant, and the caring heart of a shepherd. You will discover your calling in the Church as you serve with a giving and love-focused attitude.

If you have received your calling, continue to cultivate these qualities of the heart. The spiritual condition of your heart will directly influence your ability to grow in your calling, your capacity to understand and serve the Body of Christ. If you want to see your ministry rooted in the glory of God and the edification of the Church, your service depends on the merciful application of these heart qualities.

If you are a leader with an established ministry, tenaciously cling to the passions and values of the father's heart, the servant's heart, and the shepherd's heart. In your service as protector of your ministry and guide of God's flock, keep a close guard and watch on your own heart that it will consistently reveal the compassion, purity, and grace of the heart of Jesus.